Pass The
ENERGY,
Please!

By Barbara Shaw McKinney

Illustrated by Chad Wallace

Dawn Publications

Contents

Dedications

to Mom and Dad, for always believing in me. — BSMcK

to Mom and Dad, for supporting me and my dreams. Also special thanks to Kari Costas, Patrick Porteus, Brittany Gordon and Martha Byne for being such good models. — CW

Food manufacturing starts with a seed,
and energy waits in a plant to be freed.
Like an engine that powers the rest of a train,
a plant's the first link in an energy chain.

Each creature that feeds on a plant is a link,
absorbing energy, quick as a wink.
If that feeder, itself, becomes someone's next meal,
it lengthens the chain, like a new link of steel.

And so there's a pattern of energy passed:
a food chain has formed, first hitched to last.
Each living thing is a link in a chain
with a purpose that Nature can always explain.

Link Number One - Born in the Sun

A remarkable thing about the green plant—
it makes its own food, whereas animals can't.
Mixing carbon dioxide, water, and sun,
Mother Nature has photosynthesis fun!

A sugary food, homemade in the leaf,
travels through stems, bringing relief.
This energy needed to blossom and grow
is shared by new shoots and roots down below.

When roots reach for water, there's magic—osmosis!
Minerals pass through the roots in small doses.
These liquified vitamins found in Earth's floor
make the soil a natural health food store.

It's the same in the sea, in the watery world,
where sea-weed and kelp grow swirly and curled.
Light shining down, in merely a glimmer,
lets plants feed themselves—or some fishy swimmer.

Quite independent, on land or at sea,
a green plant produces its own energy.
Like a true power plant, the energy's stored—
green plants deserve a conservation award!

A plant by itself is a link all alone.
Its food chain future remains unknown
'til someone comes by with the greatest of ease
and firmly demands, "Pass the energy, please!"

Chains of Two – The Big Herbivore Crew

The biggest of herbivores top off their chains
by eating huge portions of grasses and grains.
Buffalo, hippos, and shy manatees
are empowered by plants in great quantities.

Saved by their size, even plant-eating dinosaurs
lived side-by-side with the meat-eating carnivores!
Gorillas love stems, and pandas, bamboo:
the links in their chains add up only to two.

Whether leaves, nuts and honey, or tender young shoots,
sweet ripened berries, flowers or fruits . . .
vegetarian power is equal in strength
to the meat found in chains of much longer length.

Energy passing from one to another
is offered by Earth to each animal brother.
A chain unbroken along the way
links plants and creatures from day to day.

Three in a Chain on the African Plain

A sea of grass on the African plain
provides for great herds with the help of the rain.
Grazing in harmony, plenty for all!
Plant power makes them grow healthy and tall.

But instinct reminds the gazelles and giraffes,
and rhinos and elephants nursing their calves,
"Beware of your neighbors. All grazers, on guard!
Carnivorous cats share your backyard!

A streamlined cheetah, designed for the chase,
runs like the wind and soon wins his race.
A graceful gazelle, nature's gift to the cat,
gives the feline a future, and he's thankful for that.

Passing the energy needed to live,
is a difficult thing for a creature to give.
But a chain unbroken along the way
links life on the plain from day to day.

A Chain of Four on the Meadow Floor

A milkweed pod explodes into seed
and parachutes down where the meadow mice feed.
A nibbling mouse gets his scamper and scurry
straight from the seed that he eats in a hurry.

But nothing's more tempting than mice on the run
to the wrigglers and squigglers who bask in the sun.
Snakes relish rodents and often depend
on mice for the slither to hunt and defend.

The satisfied snake is bulging with prey,
but danger awaits at the end of his day.
Nocturnal creatures need energy, too,
to see in the dark, to do what they do.

Alert is the owl who swivels her head
when she hears the snake rustle a leaf in his bed.
Her wide yellow eyes, designed for the night,
get their glow from the reptile, captured in flight.

Passing the energy needed to live
is a difficult gift for a creature to give.
But a chain unbroken along the way
links life in the meadow from day to day.

Arctic Five Link Up to Survive

Phytoplankton surf the sea.
They're plants adrift with energy.
Too tiny for the eye to see,
zillions float invisibly.

Now zooplankton, just slightly bigger,
gobble them up with ravenous vigor.
Power boosted by their prey,
zooplankton swim on their way.

Unaware that they've been followed,
Gone in a gulp, they're energy swallowed.
Like an "order-to-go" in an ocean deli,
they're digested in an anchovy belly.

Eventually this seafood meal
is served to a starving Arctic seal—
the energy stored is given away
to the dappled seal, all black and gray.

A risk for the seal, who pays a high price,
is a bear by a breathing hole found in the ice.
Supper will surface for polar bear
who waits for the mammal in need of air.

She thickens his blubber to wear in a storm,
and polar bear thanks her for keeping him warm.
Fattening up in the Arctic so cold,
gives chubby young cubs a chance to grow old.

Passing the energy needed to live
is a difficult gift for a creature to give.
But a chain unbroken along the way
links life in the Arctic from day to day.

Woodland Mix Makes Chain of Six

Goldenrod growing all mustard and green
is a natural, magical food machine.
When the plant, full of chlorophyll, captures some sun,
energy's born, and the food chain's begun.

Caterpillar looking for a luscious lunch,
spots the plant with its crispy crunch.
While chomping away on his leafy treat,
power is passed to his six pairs of feet.

To a spider in search of a scrumptious snack,
the plump leggy worm is ripe for attack.
She spins a silk dragline and drops from a daisy;
full from her supper, soon she feels lazy.

A warbler waits in the brush on a branch,
watching for spider to give her a chance.
She swoops on the spider, so thankful indeed
for a heartier meal than a seed from a weed.

At the edge of the wood a weasel is walking—
slinking in shadows, he's really out stalking.
There's not enough time for the songbird to fly!
She gives him swiftness and keenness of eye.

Watch out, Mr. Weasel. Who lurks at your back?
A sly red fox is hot on your track!
The weasel is energy just within reach;
her pups share the prey, a portion for each.

Passing the energy needed to live,
is a difficult thing for a creature to give.
But a chain unbroken along the way
links life in the woodland from day to day.

Decomposers on the Ground—
Nutrients Go Round and Round

The animal giants have little to fear,
for very few enemies dare to come near.
But even top predators, king of their chains,
feed hungry scavengers with their remains.

The vulture is known as a great opportunist
that preys on the fallen if finding it soonest.
An energy source does not go to waste—
it's passed to each creature that fights for a taste.

Beetles attracted to carcass and dung
quickly bury their treasure—it's food for their young!
And maggots from blowflies will eat all they can,
whereas ants store their hoard till hungry again.

Moths feed on hairs and lay eggs on the site.
Their larvae won't have to look far for a bite.
They'll find enough energy needed to skitter,
while cleaning up nature's most natural litter.

No visible signs remain of the beast,
but living things wait in the soil to feast.
Something called fungus with tangly thread
absorbs even more from the flesh of the dead.

And millions of microscopic bacteria
attack what's left over in Earth's cafeteria.
Earthworms then gobble and tunnel below,
and mix it all up so that new plants can grow.

As energy's shared by the great and the small,
each break-down releases the best gift of all—
to the soil some nutrients make their escape,
and the "circle of life" takes its wonderful shape!

All Nature's creatures, linked in some way,
are returned to the ground in the form of decay.
But their energy lives, like souls, in the Earth,
that nurture new life and cycle new birth.

Ecosystems will only survive
if balanced food chains keep species alive.
Too much of this, too little of that,
threatens a healthy habitat.

We endanger the creatures by taking their space—
they can't make their homes in the natural place.
Their food sources dwindle, they die of starvation,
and food chains are weakened, a bad situation.

Let's learn from the creatures,
the wisest of teachers,
who pass their energy, one to another,
respecting and trusting their Planet Earth Mother.

Barbara Shaw McKinney writes about the "big ideas" in nature in an effort to help children understand the world and their special role in it. As a poet, she writes to inspire young independent learners at home and in school. As an Instructional Resource Teacher in East Hartford, Connecticut, she is committed to helping children become lifelong readers and writers. *Pass the Energy, Please!* is her second book. Both it and her first book, *A Drop Around the World*, celebrate the gift of life and remind us to be thankful for the contributions of each and every living thing on Earth.

Chad Wallace is a young artist who created the oil paintings in this book at age twenty-four. He was raised and lives in Westchester County, New York, and has a cabin at Bear Mountain where he sometimes does art and always gets inspiration. He loves to hike and camp, and has worked as a youth activities director. Chad received a Bachelor of Fine Arts in illustration from Syracuse University's School of Visual and Performing Arts.

Copyright © 1999 Barbara Shaw McKinney
Illustrations copyright © 1999 Chad Wallace

A Sharing Nature With Children Book

Library of Congress Cataloging-in-Publication Data

McKinney, Barbara Shaw, 1951-
    Pass the energy, please! / by Barbara Shaw McKinney; illustrated by Chad Wallace. – 1st ed.
        p. cm. – (A Sharing nature with children book)
        Summary: Rhyming text and illustrations present nature's food chains, from a simple seed to a top predator, demonstrating their natural links.
        ISBN: 1-58469-001-1 (case)
        ISBN: 1-58469-002-X (paper)

1. Food chains (Ecology) Juvenile literature. [1. Food chains (Ecology) 2. Ecology.] I. Wallace, Chad, ill. II. Title. III. Series.
QH541.14.M37   2000
577'.16—dc21   99-32181 CIP

Printed in China

10 9 8 7 6 5 4 3 2

First Edition
Design by Andrea Miles
Computer production by Rob Froelick

Dawn Publications
Post Office Box 2010
Nevada City, CA 95959
800-545-7475
Email: nature@dawnpub.com
Website: wwwdawnpub.com

AVAILABLE: A TEACHER'S GUIDE

A Teacher's Guide to Nature's Food Chain, by Carol Malnor, is a companion to *Pass the Energy, Please!* It explains how to create dynamic learning centers based on the various food chains. Different types of food chains, habitats, and animal relationships are explored using approaches that incorporate multiple intelligences including movement, art, music, writing, and math activity centers for both individual and group work.

ALSO BY BARBARA SHAW MCKINNEY

A Drop Around the World, by Barbara Shaw McKinney, illustrated by Michael Maydak, follows a single drop of water—from snow to steam, from polluted to purified, from stratus cloud to subterranean crack. Drop inspires our respect for water's unique role on Earth. (Teacher's Guide available.)

OTHER DISTINCTIVE NATURE AWARENESS BOOKS FROM DAWN PUBLICATIONS

My Monarch Journal, by Connie Muther, shows in stunning photography the metamorphosis of a tiny egg to a caterpillar, then to a chrysalis, and finally to a beautiful butterfly. It is also a journal in which students follow the development of their own monarch, with ample space for notes, drawings and charts, stimulating a profound appreciation for these remarkable tiny beings. Available in both student (32 p.) and parent-teacher (52 p.) editions.

With Love, to Earth's Endangered Peoples, by Virginia Kroll. All over the world, groups of people, like species of animals, are endangered. Often these people have a beautiful, meaningful relationship with the Earth, and with each other. This book portrays several of these groups of people, with love. (Teacher's Guide available.)

Lifetimes, by David Rice, introduces some of nature's longest, shortest, and most unusual lifetimes, and what they have to teach us. This book teaches, but it also goes right to the heart. (Teacher's Guide available.)

A Walk in the Rainforest, A Swim through the Sea, and A Fly in the Sky—the popular trilogy of habitat books written and illustrated by the young author, Kristin Joy Pratt. Each book presents its habitat in alphabetical and alliterative format. (Teacher's Guides available for each book.)

A Tree in the Ancient Forest, by Carol Reed-Jones, uses repetitive, cumulative verse to show graphically the remarkable web of interdependent plants and animals that all call a big old tree home.

The Sharing Nature With Children Series of Teacher's Guides is distinctive in that they integrate character education with core science and language arts curricula.

Dawn Publications is dedicated to inspiring in children a deeper understanding and appreciation for all life on Earth. To order, or for a copy of our catalog, please call 800-545-7475. You may also order, view the catalog, see reviews and much more online at www.dawnpub.com.